SIGMUND KALINA
# Three Drops of Water
illustrated by Charles Robinson

Lothrop, Lee & Shepard Company / New York

*Other Good Books by Sigmund Kalina*

The House That Nature Built
Air, the Invisible Ocean
Your Bones Are Alive
Your Nerves and Their Messages

Text copyright © 1974 by Sigmund Kalina
Illustrations copyright © 1974 by Charles Robinson
All rights reserved. No part of this book may be
reproduced or utilized in any form or by any means, electronic
or mechanical, including photocopying, recording or by
any information retrieval system, without permission in writing
from the Publisher. Inquiries should be addressed to Lothrop,
Lee and Shepard Company, 105 Madison Ave., New York,
N.Y. 10016. Printed in the United States of America.

3 4 5

Kalina, Sigmund.
 Three drops of water.

 1. Fresh—water biology—Juvenile literature.
2. Stream ecology—Juvenile literature. 3. Water-Pollution—
Juvenile literature. I. Robinson, Charles,
(date) illus. II. Title.
QH96.16.K34 574.5′2632 73-12468
ISBN 0-688-41547-4
ISBN 0-688-51547-9 (lib. bdg.)

To my esteemed uncle,
Dr. Emanuel Kalina—
completely and unselfishly dedicated
to his patients

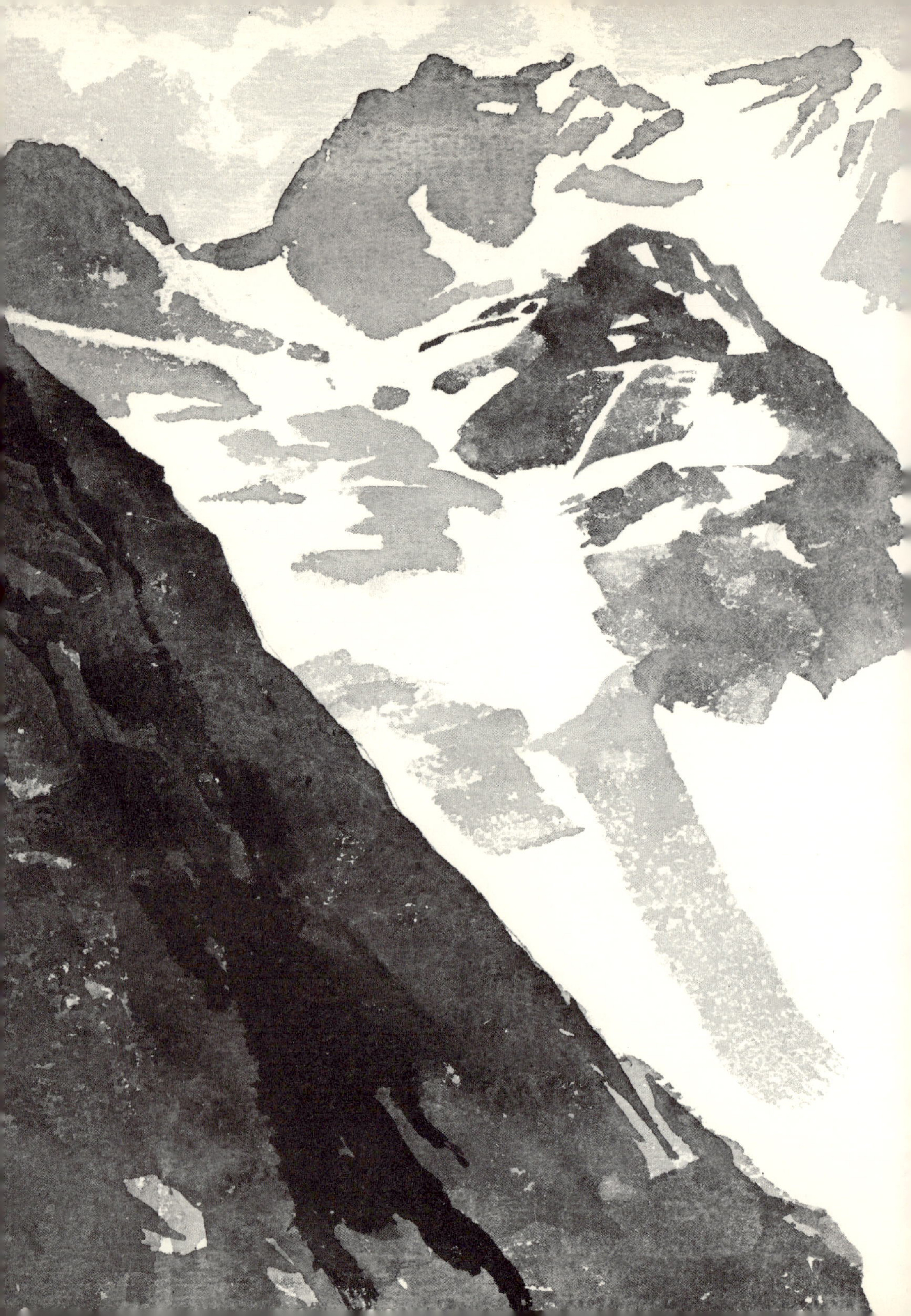

**H**igh on the mountain, it is cold—
so cold that there is always snow.
Season after season, the
fallen winter snow is pressed
into a huge thick sheet of ice.

But in the spring, the top ice layers
begin to melt.
Drip . . . drip . . . drip . . .
three drops of water trickle down
the wall of a deep
wide crack in the ice.

Before long, the fresh water
locked inside the ice
begins to seep out from underneath.
Our three drops of water
are now free to flow toward the sea.

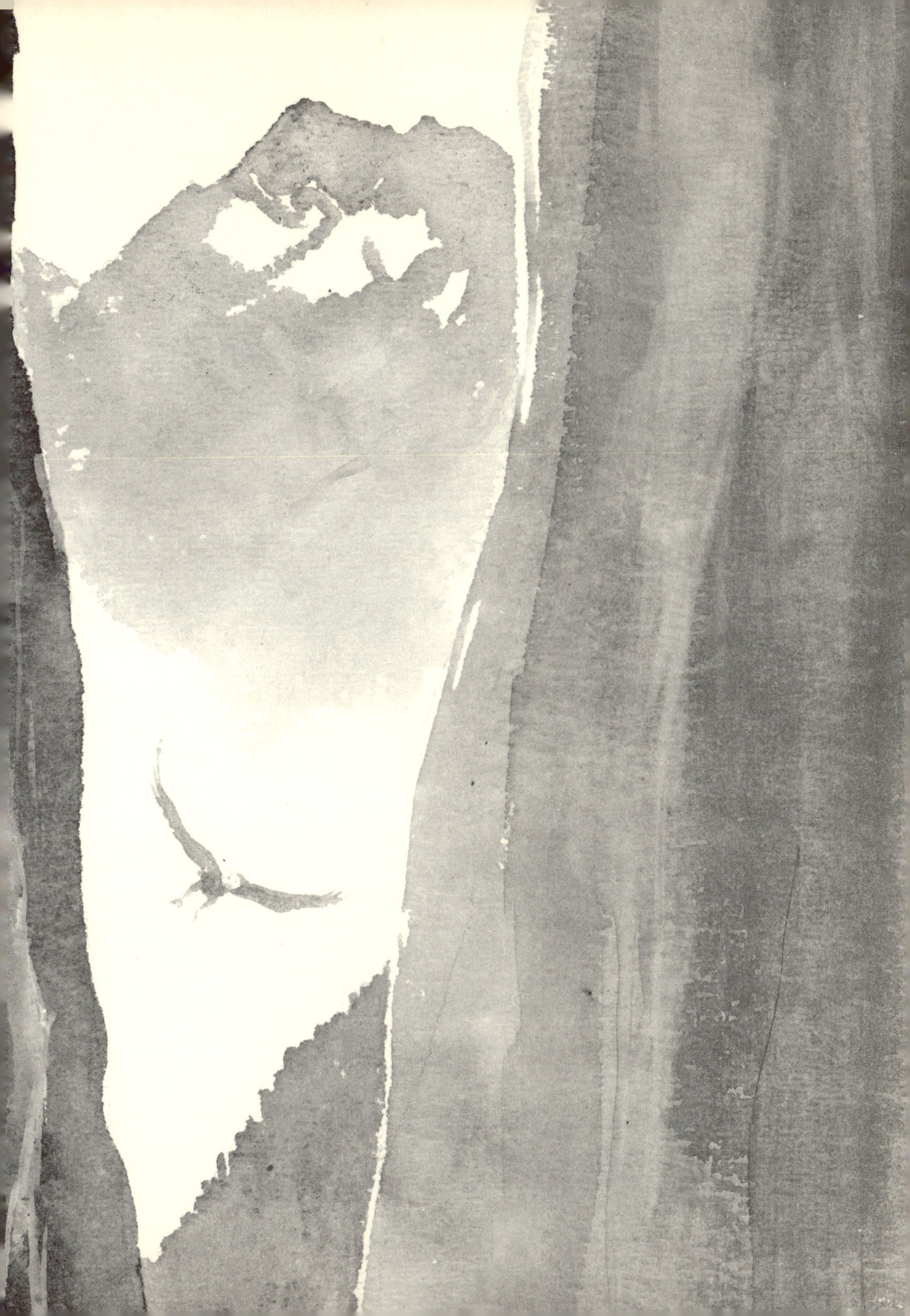

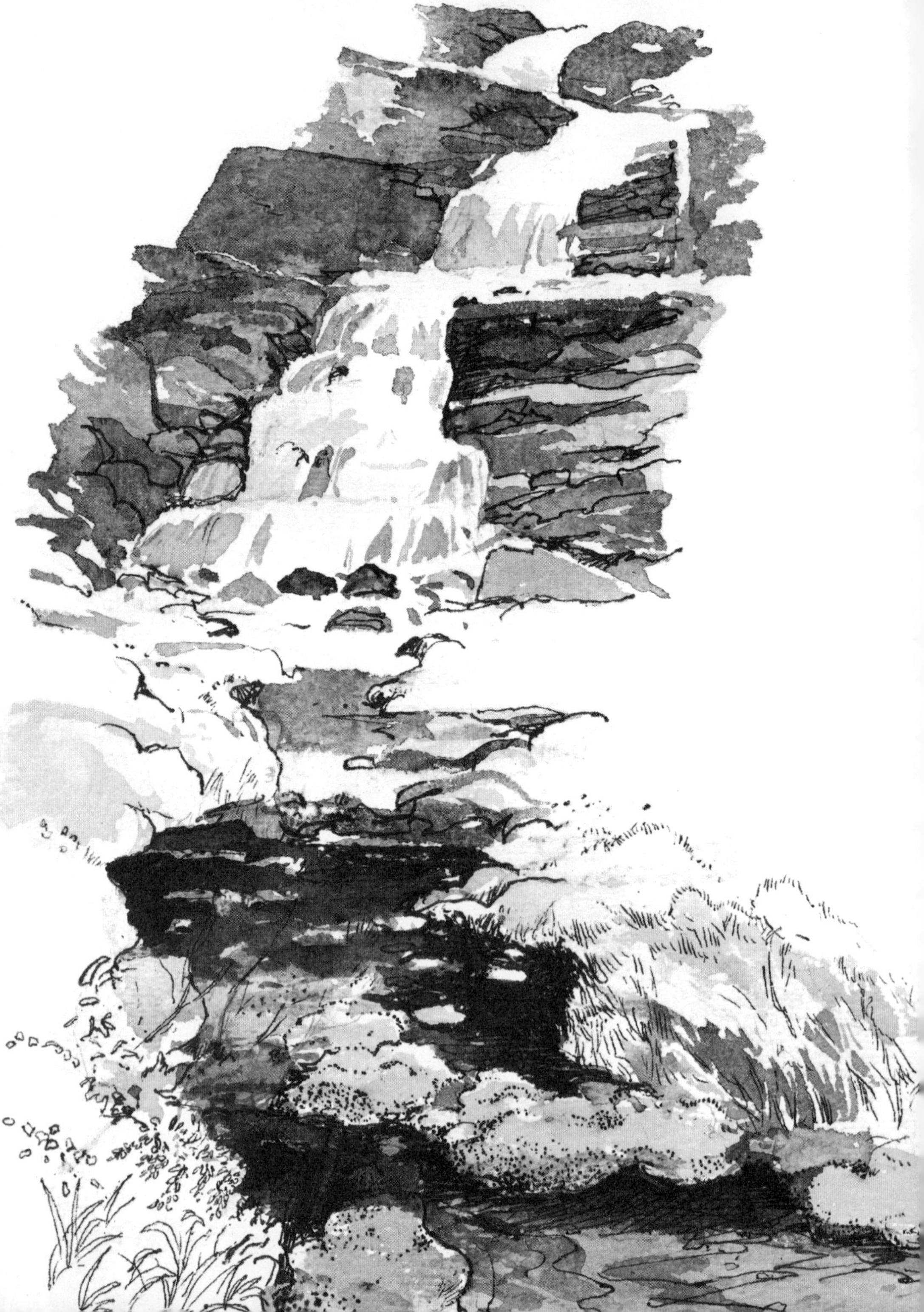

Miles later, the thin stream
is joined by waters coming down
from mountain lakes and trickling
out of deep-cracked rocks.
Ripples of water race down
the mountainside.

The small stream has now become
a young brook, its banks bordered
with clumps of grass-like plants
and moss-covered rocks.

Threadlike green plants cling
to the rocks, forming a network where algae,
the tiniest of green plants,
can make their home.
In this way, young plant life
is anchored down, saved from being
washed away in the strong swift currents.

The streamlined bodies
of young growing fish swim against
the strong pull of the rushing brook.
Darting from rock to rock, they are
kept safe from the swift current.

Nature has designed some insects
with clinging parts to help them
live in these hurrying waters.
One insect is the black fly.
Before a black fly is born,
it changes from an egg to a blackish
rod-shaped speck called a larva.
In some places, there are so many
black-fly larvae that the rocks
seem to be covered with black velvet.

Larvae are always hungry. They stick
to the rocks with tiny sucking pads,
and hold up two hairlike fans
which wave in the currents.
This is how the larvae trap their food.
They feed on bits of floating algae.

12

Every animal must eat,
and each animal, in turn,
may be eaten by another animal.
Larvae feed on algae,
fish feed on the larvae,
and big fish feed upon small fish.
This is called a "food chain."
It is nature's way of making certain
that each creature in these waters
gets its share of food.

Where the brook is not deep,
rocks jut up from the pebbled bottom.
Around these rocks, the rushing stream
bubbles into white foam.
Here, oxygen from the air mixes
more easily with the stirred-up waters.

Nature has invented special breathing
structures called gills
for the many water-living animals.

The next time you catch a fish,
gently lift its gill covers.
You will see thin red featherlike
layers, one on top of another.
These are the gills.
Gills work for a fish
as your lungs work for you.

In breathing, your lungs make it
possible for you to capture the oxygen
mixed in with the inhaled air.
When a fish "breathes," it uses
its gills, which are specially designed
to capture the oxygen mixed in
with the water.

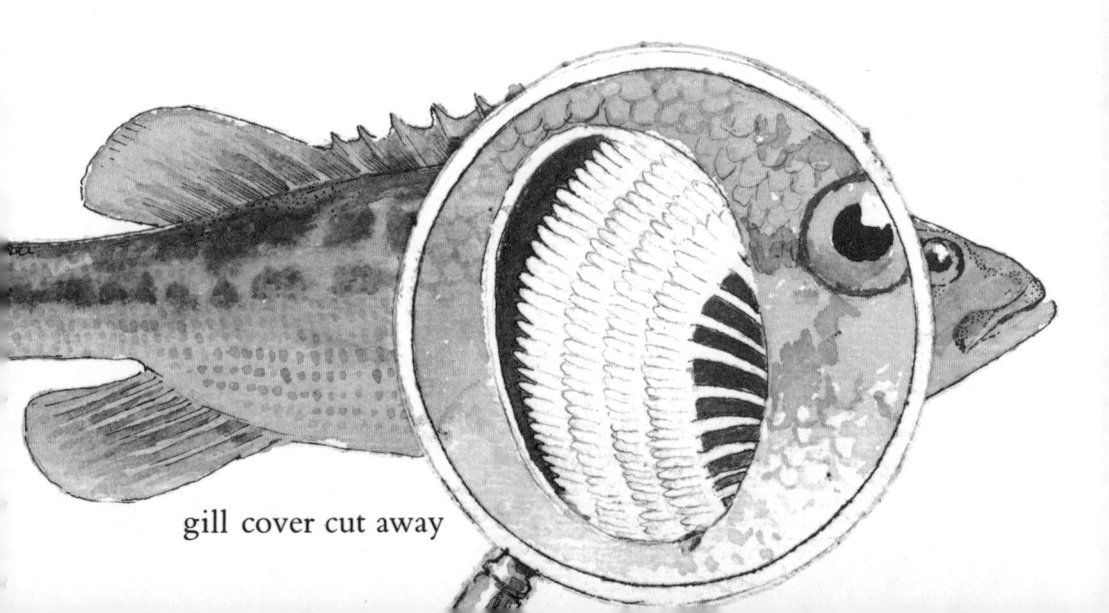

gill cover cut away

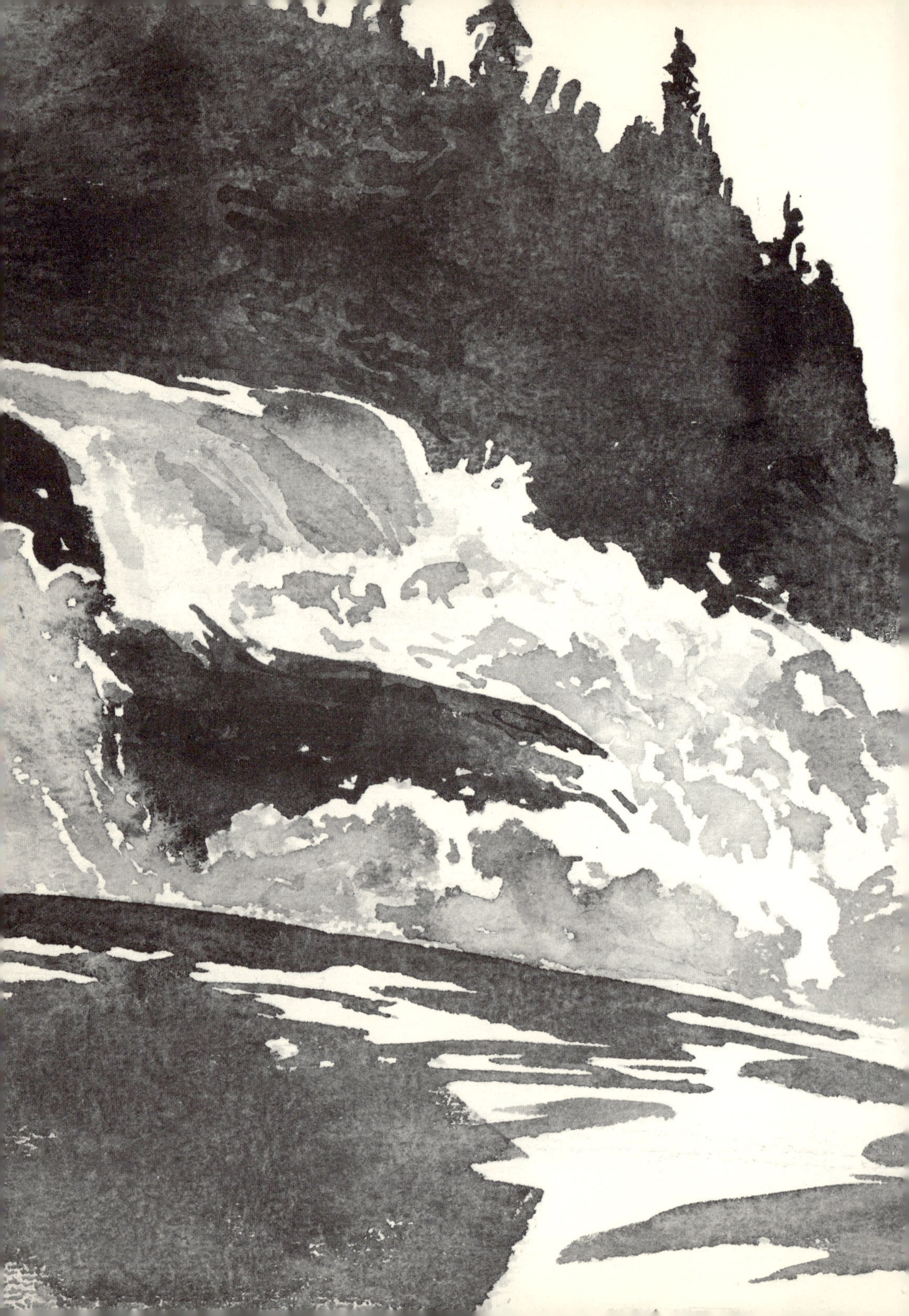

In this mountain brook world,
nature provides enough food,
plenty of oxygen, and a generous
supply of clean water.
Here, plants and animals lead
healthy lives.
The water keeps sweeping its way
downstream over a bed of shiny rocks.
Nothing has a chance to stay in one
place and rot.

Our three drops of water,
caught up in this fresh mountain stream,
continue their journey toward the sea.
After miles of turning and tumbling
over the rocks, the young brook leaves
the mountainside. With a sudden bend,
it comes upon a companion stream.

For a short distance, the two streams flow side by side, with a thin wedge of earth separating them.
Downriver, the sandy ridge soon wears away and disappears.
The two streams become one. Stretches of green land greet the newborn river on both sides.

The moving waters cut through open
fields fringed with tangles of willows
and wooded shrubs.
Softened brown earth gives way to the
onrushing stream. Soil, sand, and tiny
pebbles come sliding down into the
hurrying waters.

Before long, the land begins to flatten.
The river slows down, snaking its way along
in wide loops and horseshoe bends.
Wherever it rubs against the land,
more earth and stones wash away.
The widening river, with its
slow-moving waters clouded by millions of
rubbed-off soil particles,
darkens to a muddy brown.

Algae and leafy underwater plants,
sunken branches and water soaked logs,
darken the bottom in quiet mystery.
Our three drops of water
have now become
part of a sluggish winding river.

Below the surface, green pond weeds
thicken into a jungle where fish
can hide and hunt for food.
The sandy bottom is crowded with
very small mussels, sticking
halfway out of the mud.
Their soft bodies are protected by
a pair of hinged shells
about a quarter of an inch long.

With their shells slightly open,
these tiny creatures feed by
pumping water in and out.
Usually mussels live in clean waters.
When the water becomes polluted,
mussels clamp their shells tight
and dig deeper into the mud.
They cannot live this way very long,
because they are unable to breathe
or feed through their closed shells.
This does not happen to fish;
fish swim away.

In nature, no river is "pure."
Fish cannot live in pure water.
They need clean water—
water with enough oxygen, enough food,
and with no harmful chemicals.

Our river is very much alive
with dense cushions of algae,
hungry insect larvae, and creeping snails.
Clean water sweeps through open
mussel shells, and bathes the
delicate gills of fish hidden among
the water weeds.

Many miles downstream, the land
alongside the river changes.
The green lacework of jumbled shrubs
gives way to open fields of
corn and wheat.
A hint of trouble is in sight for
our three drops of water
as the river wanders through
the surrounding farmland.

Many a farmer uses chemical sprays
to keep insects and their hungry larvae
from eating and spoiling his crops.
When it rains, the chemicals clinging
to the plants are washed into the ground.
The underground water tunnels through
the earth and carries its load
of chemicals into the river.

Before long, algae, insect larvae, and a host of tiny bottom-dwelling creatures become poisoned.
Since they are food for river fish, the fish begin to suffer and soon disappear.

The exploring river zigzags through
the mountains. This is coal country.
Here, rocks along the river's edge
are caked with bright yellow deposits.
Gone is the healthy green
of growing moss.

Unclean reddish-brown flakes
settle along the river bottom.
The water appears to be turning orange;
an unpleasant odor hangs in the air.
Something is wrong!

Deep inside forgotten coal mines,
harmful acids seep into underground waters.
The oozing acid water finds its way
into the river, making it unhealthful
for plants and animals living there.

Fish can tell when there are
harmful chemicals spoiling the water.
They can taste the tiniest
change in the water.
And they are known to have
a strong sense of smell.
Scientists believe that many fish,
when hunting for food,
can smell their way to places
where plants are growing in the river.

This part of the river is
truly in trouble.
Fish leave for cleaner waters.
Bottom-crawling bugs,
mud-scooping larvae,
and tiny digging clams soon disappear,
along with the dying plant life.
A few threadlike algae remain.

Leaving the mountain coal country behind,
our three drops of water
continue downstream.
No longer does the river turn.
Like a ribbon, it unwinds straight ahead
into a busy town emptying
greasy wastes into the waters.

There is no turning back for
the river waters as they reach
the outskirts of the town
where many factories, hard at work,
are waiting for them.

There is a huge paper mill.
Though it is hidden by the high
sandy bank of the river, you
can tell that it is there.
A horrible odor fills the air.
It smells like a million rotten eggs.

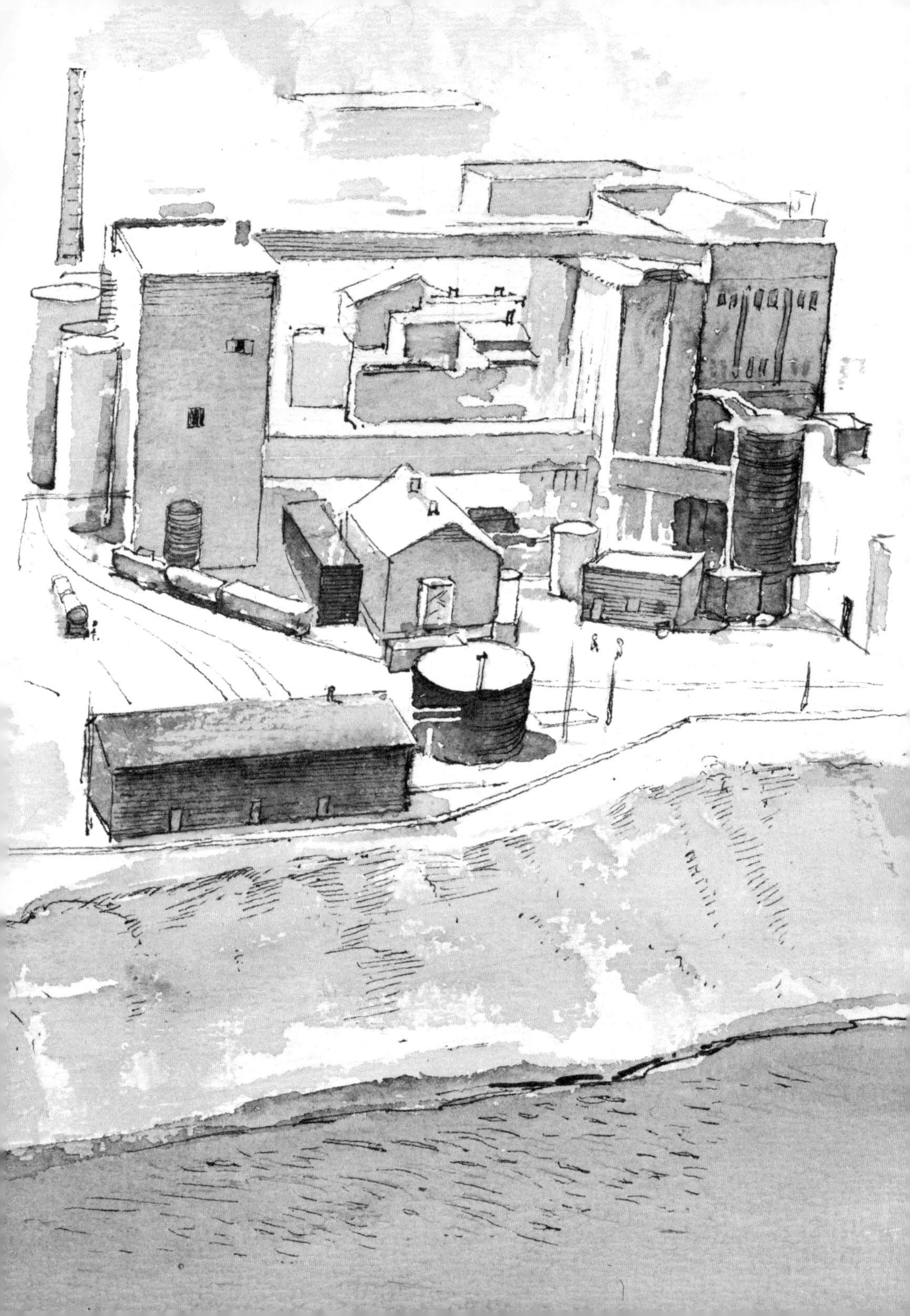

Paper mills need lots of water.
To make one ton of paper,
it takes more than two hundred tons
of water!
Very hot steam and water help peel
the bark and clean the soft tree wood.
The bare wood is chipped into bits
that look like cereal.
More water is used to wash
the wood pulp.
Along with the returning water,
a mess of stringy fibers is dumped
into the river.

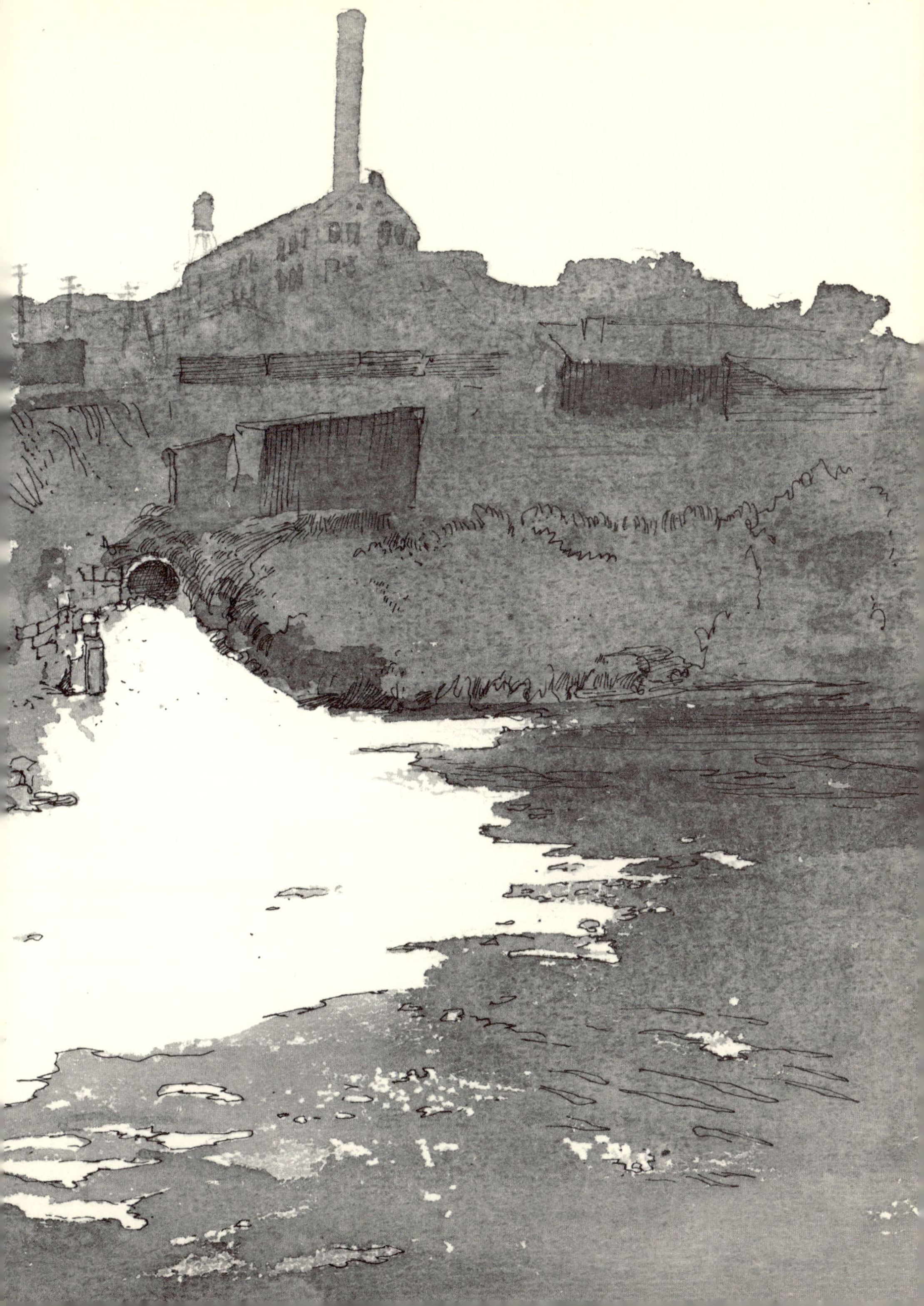

Tons of fibers continue emptying into the river. Some catch onto rocks and cling there.

Some fibers settle slowly to the bottom.
Others are so light, they hang in the water.
The river becomes clouded with a web
of cotton-like fibers.
The fibers are not poisonous,
but they can be harmful in other ways.
They block the light from reaching
the bottom. Light-starved plants soon die.
The many animals that use these plants
for food and a place to hide
are now in trouble.

Although the fibers are soft,
they can scratch the delicate gills
of fish and mussels.
Very often, these clinging fibers
almost cover the gills,
keeping them from being bathed
by the oxygen-filled waters.
Because of this, the fish and mussels
find it hard to breathe.

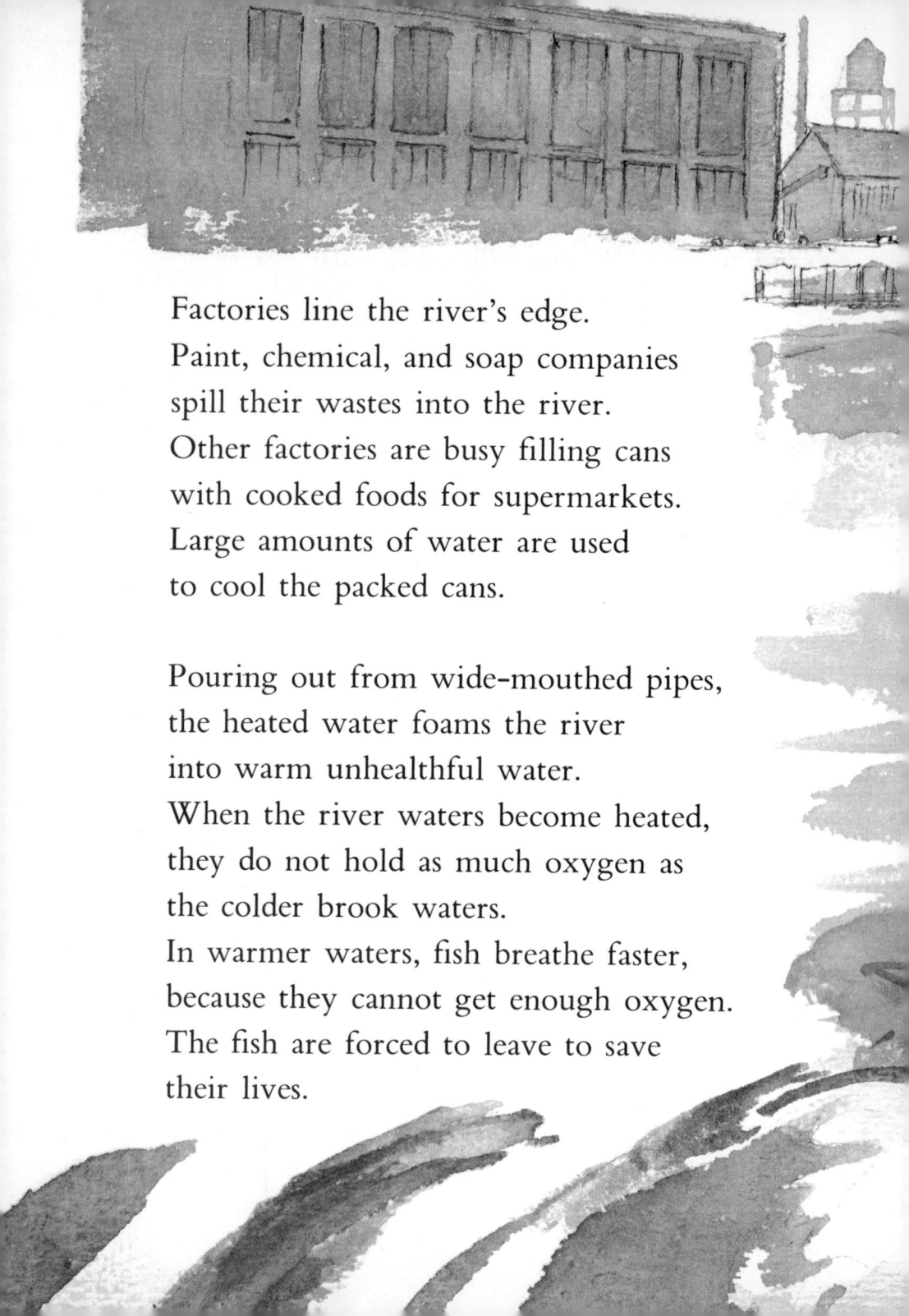

Factories line the river's edge.
Paint, chemical, and soap companies
spill their wastes into the river.
Other factories are busy filling cans
with cooked foods for supermarkets.
Large amounts of water are used
to cool the packed cans.

Pouring out from wide-mouthed pipes,
the heated water foams the river
into warm unhealthful water.
When the river waters become heated,
they do not hold as much oxygen as
the colder brook waters.
In warmer waters, fish breathe faster,
because they cannot get enough oxygen.
The fish are forced to leave to save
their lives.

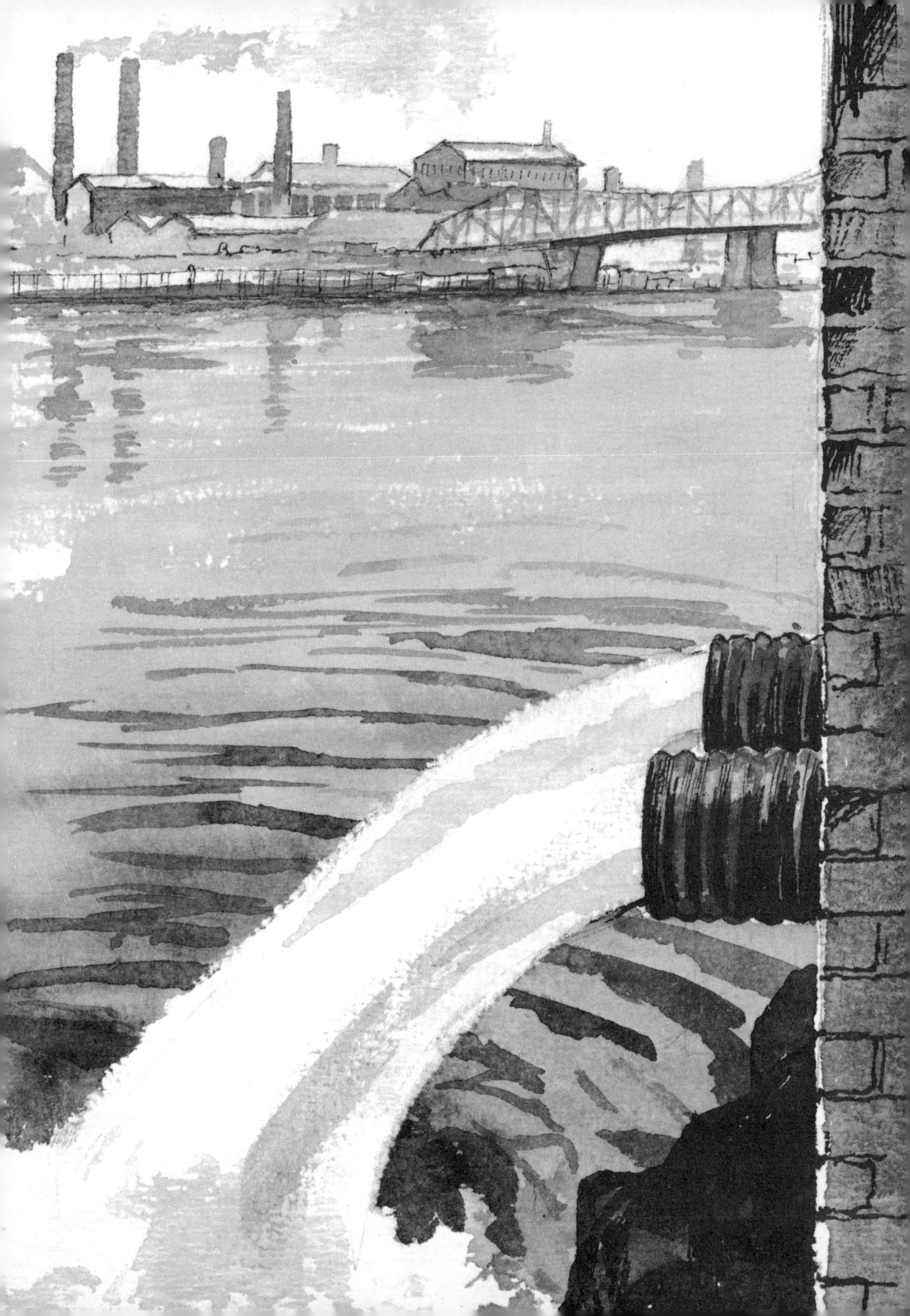

A few miles downstream,
our three drops of water slow down,
as the river thickens with more mud.
Giant bulldozers chew up the land,
while dusting winds and heavy rains
wash the loosened earth into the river.

Heavy particles of soil find their
way to the bottom.
Many nests of fish eggs are buried.
A blanket of mud soon smothers
the animals living there.
The river world darkens.

Without light, green plants cannot
manufacture the food upon which
so much of the hungry river life depends.
And the oxygen which is always given off
is missing from these murky waters.

The community of animals living in this oxygen-starved river changes. Gone are the bright frisky darting fish. Hugging the bottom are thick, large-scaled fish having brown bodies tinged with orange.

These fish are carp.
Unlike most fish, carp can live
in water with less oxygen.
Carp are not fussy eaters.
They poke at the muddy bottom, searching
for food other fish will not eat.
Tiny worms, dead fish, and insects
are part of the carp's diet.

No longer do we find mussels.
They need clean water.
New visitors are now seen wiggling
in the mud bottom.
Worms, no longer than half an inch
and no thicker than a sewing needle,
tunnel in the muddy floor of the river.

Scientists call these cousins of
the earthworm "sludgeworms."
The blood of sludgeworms,
just like yours, is red.
There are so many of them, the bottom
of the river becomes covered
with patches of soft red cushions . . .
alive with wiggling threadlike tails.
This is a sign of unhealthy water.

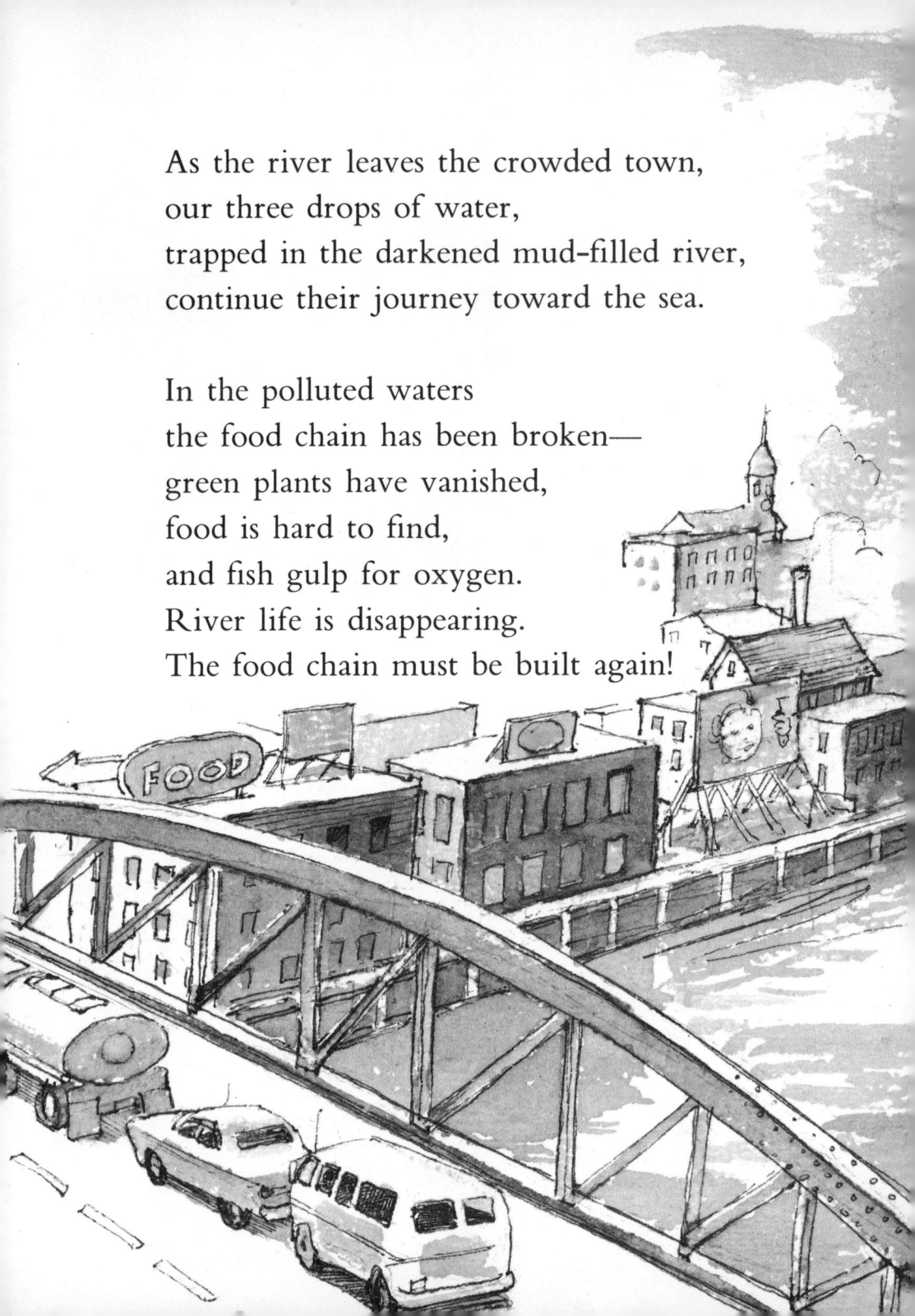

As the river leaves the crowded town,
our three drops of water,
trapped in the darkened mud-filled river,
continue their journey toward the sea.

In the polluted waters
the food chain has been broken—
green plants have vanished,
food is hard to find,
and fish gulp for oxygen.
River life is disappearing.
The food chain must be built again!

Nature has a way of helping troubled waters.
A river can clean itself, given enough time to travel a long distance, and enough fresh water flowing in.

The first thing our sick river
needs back again is certain bacteria that
feed on things that were once alive—
dead fish, dead plants, and garbage
of all kinds.
Bacteria make these things decay.

When paper, wood fibers, dead worms,
or dead water weeds begin to
break down and rot,
body-building nitrogen compounds
are released and dissolve in the water.
This is nature's method of
fertilizing her food-starved rivers.
Nitrogen is good for growing plants.

Slowly the river begins to show
a hint of healthy green.
A garden of algae starts to grow.
Other plants soon follow.
Once the green plant life returns,
more oxygen is given off by the
busy food-making plants.

The food chain has now begun. Once again,
creeping snails and hungry larvae
begin feasting on the growing algae.
Small fish feed on the fattened larvae.
Big fish, hiding among the water weeds,
wait quietly for their dinner
of small fish.

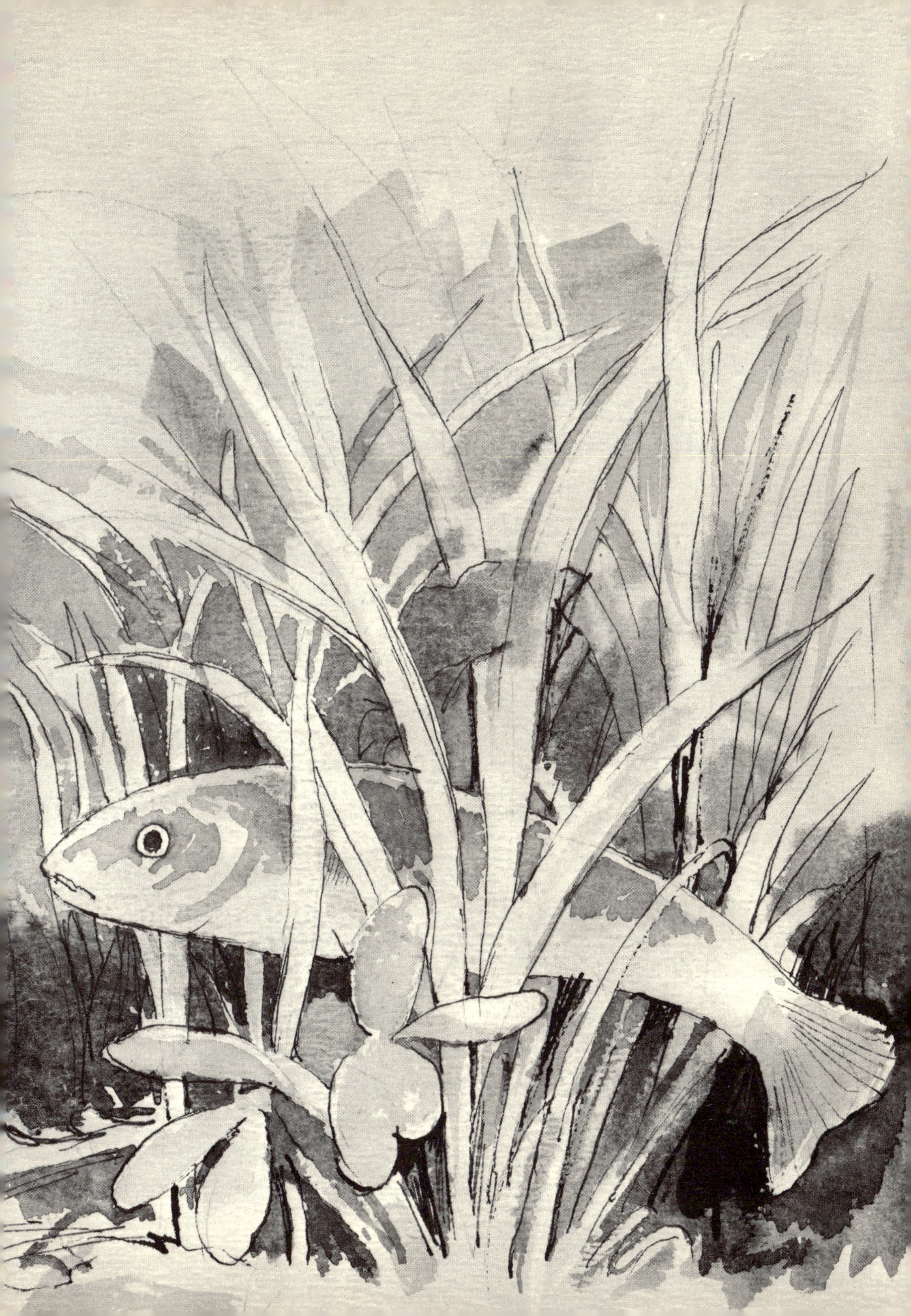

The river bottom has lost its
dirty slime. Tiny clams and mussels
peek out of a cleaner and
sandy river bed. Their open shells
suck in fresh clean water.
Sunlight streaks through the water.
A small sunfish escapes the
sharp beak of a diving kingfisher.
The river community shows signs
of renewed life.

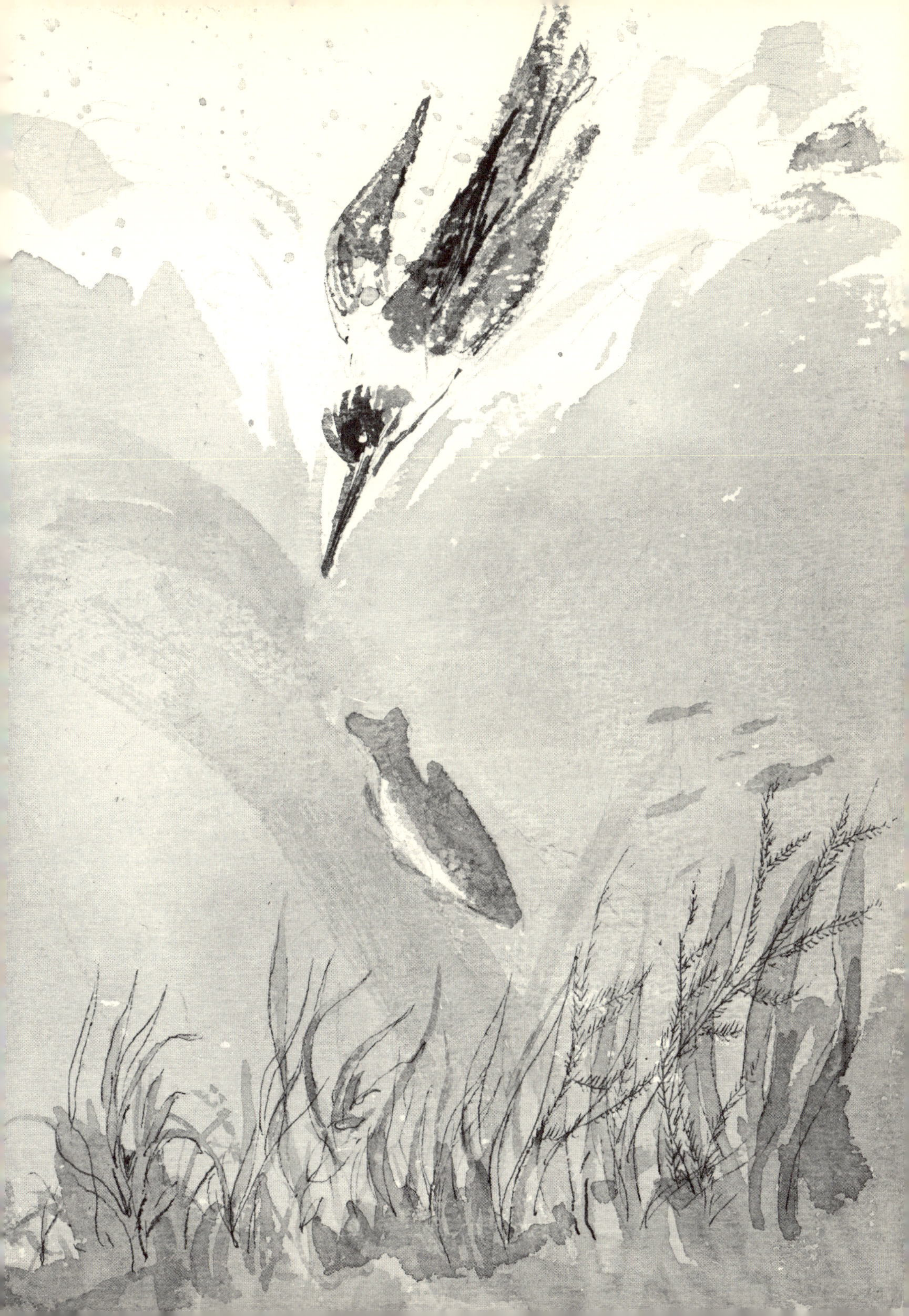

Our three drops of water
are nearing the end of their journey.
The seacoast is not far off.

Suddenly the waters seem to be
hemmed in. Slowly they wind their way
between islands of marshland
topped with spikes
of coarse grass known as cord grass.

Our river now helps bathe
the salt marshes where it meets and mixes
with the waters from the sea.
Here, in quiet ponds fenced in by
tall grasses, traveling ducks stop to rest
and feed their young.
Here, away from the churning ocean waves,
many fish from the sea
seek safe nesting places to lay their eggs.

Indeed, these salt marshes are nature's own nurseries, used by many animals seeking protection for their young.

Incoming tides stir the quiet
salt-marsh waters with more oxygen.
Outgoing tides, rich with decaying
particles of plants and animals,
mix with the open sea to become

part of food chains in ocean waters.
Marshes are important.
They are the gateways through which flows much of the health-giving food needed by the variety of ocean life.

With the outgoing tides from the marsh,
our three drops of water
are swept into the sea.
Gusting winds curl the ocean top
into fountains of mist disappearing
into the air.

Caught up in the evaporating spray,
our three drops are borne aloft
with the changing winds.

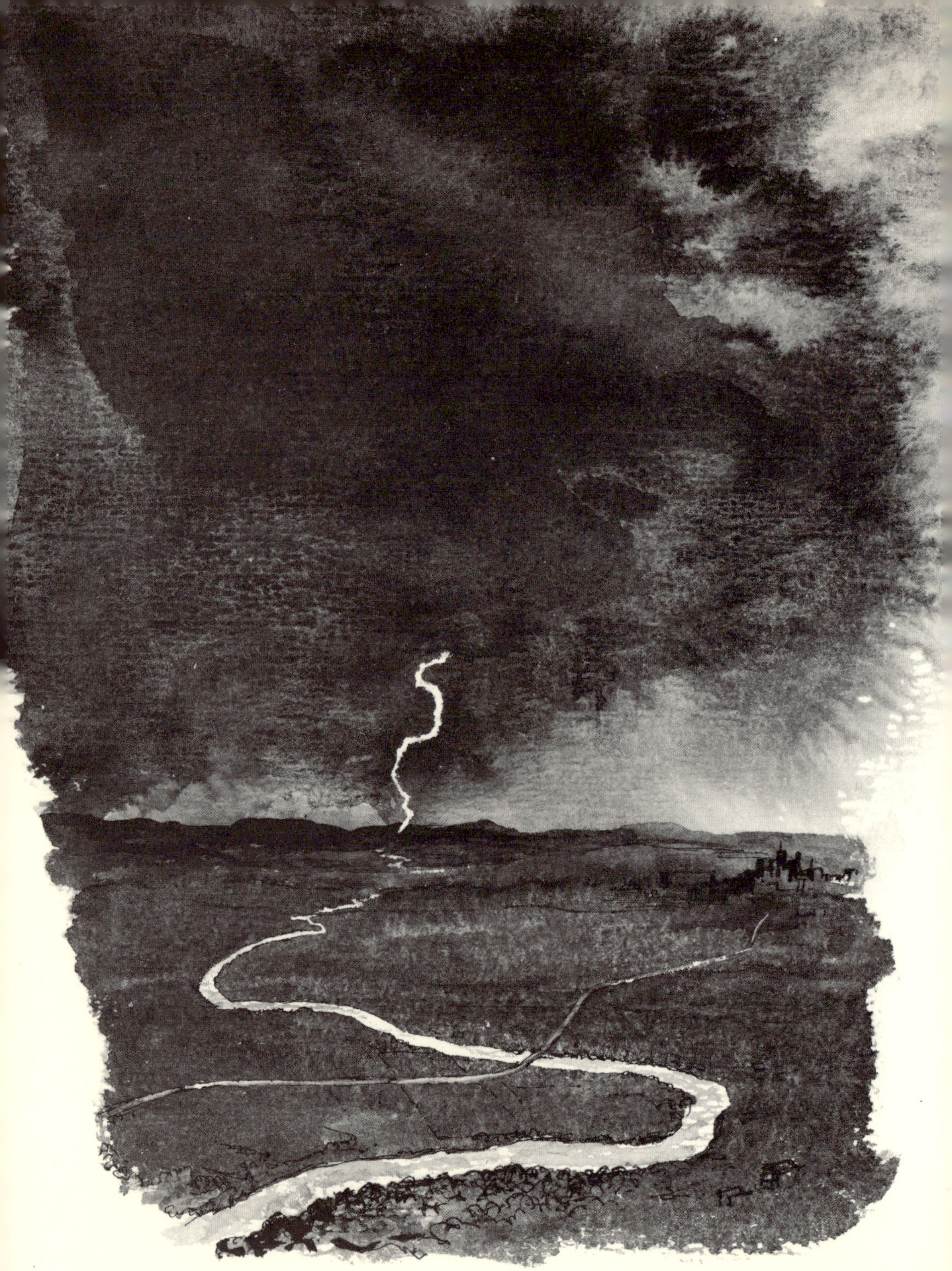

One drop, perhaps trapped inside
a darkened thundercloud, soon plunges
into a river a hundred miles away.

The second drop, also imprisoned
in the cloud, lands on a soft leaf
and falls to the earth.
It is not long before it is
sucked in by a thirsty root.

Our third drop of water, blown far up north,
freezes into a tiny lacy snowflake.
Drifting down with the falling snow,
it becomes lost again in the ice,
high on the mountain.